Words as They Fell into Line

A Book of Formal Verse

by

Susan Rebecca Wetmore

Finishing Line Press
Georgetown, Kentucky

Words as They Fell into Line

A Book of Formal Verse

ACKNOWLEDGMENTS

Publisher: Leah Huete de Maines
Editor: Christen Kincaid
Cover Art: Susan Rebecca Wetmore
Author Photo: Susan Rebecca Wetmore
Cover Design: Elizabeth Maines McCleavy

Order online: www.finishinglinepress.com

Author inquiries and mail orders:
Finishing Line Press
P. O. Box 1626
Georgetown, Kentucky 40324
U. S. A.

Table of Contents

To B.M.M.C., with thanks.

Mirrored

Pale, narrow mirror in this narrow room,
Hung opposite the single window's view
To echo daylight within indoor gloom.

Glum mimic, whose clear skies were greyish blue,
Where lilacs bloomed as drab as dusty lace,
Dim clouds dropped murky rain, and stale winds blew.

If mirrors opened, I could reach my face
To drown my nose in those soaked lilac blooms
That were themselves, and not reflected grace.

Fresh

Come breathe, the sluggish air still smells of night.
Cold raindrops ornament a spider's web
Among thorned shrubs
That drip with light.

Well, don't you like this prettiness? Your wet
Shoes chill and chafe your soles. Your day ahead's
A half-seen dread,
Like spider's net.

Night

Ice glitter falls from clear still air, sparkles
In streetlights underneath cold skies of stars.

Daybreak

More quietly than night fell breaks this dawn,
As indeterminate as lint. Sheer curtains
Veil the early sidewalk, vague, uncertain.

Daylight

Blank sky in day's glare seems
As empty as the sight
Of endless sea, though teems
With lighted ships at night.

Window

Across the screen, shrunk tendrils poke
Their knobs. A young, translucent vine
Once shuttered here and still entwines,
As it would not release, but broke.

Where

Beyond this windowsill, its crusted vase,
Its dried out leaf that shatters, where are you?
Not here, not this room, these steps, this blank space.
But, are you mendable, with thread, with glue?

Sun

Bare sunlight slants, details
Shadows of trees and grazing
Light focuses pale
Highlights on cross-lit things.

Late Summer Haiku

Cold wet sand and air.
This hour, chill ghosts of autumn
Drift next to water.

Hiking In Late Autumn Haiku

Threadbare November,
Faded pale like fading sun,
Wear it yet, but freeze.

Flower Haiku

Gardenias bloom white,
But blossoms plunge pungencies
Bold-hued as garnet.

Fall

Fall sun sets; aspens, clouds aglow.
Lone jogger's loping like a rider,
Edging fields that reek like cider,
And the headwind smells like snow.

Forgotten

If someone wears your coat, your specs,
A brief heart's beat I'll pause, expect
Delicious chat, expect your grin,
Think he is you, before you thinned
And died. Ideas I'd share, cannot
Because you're gone, though I'd forgot.

Thaw

When spring strips nude of snow the trash
Of all a winter, bares regrets
In mud, then comes squelched warmth and brash
Green leaves upholster flowerbeds.

February

Adoring valentine swears not to part
'Til all the beer runs green, and deftly plays
That pagan Roman prank of Cupid's darts,
With palm fronds, flowers, candle, cleft chin, praise,
Red satin heart. De-canonized, no martyr.

Affair

Tall lady, flicking spinet, twisting noise,
Forced into modes, squirming her own high voice
From cadence of calm speech to flowing airs.
Her form, which clothing both distorts and bares,
Swells wine-bruised velvet, swooning velvet skin.
Base loyalty's for serfs, free pride's in treason.

Scents

My muted, muffled perfume, may I ask,
This pout? Aloof? Here, where you're so adored!

Rich fragrance wafts unchanged from this glass flask,
It's your spoiled nose that's dullened, numb, and bored.

Muse

I live and breathe. I breathe and whiff
The air. And if that's all I'd ask?
Solid profession? Only if
I'd had the foresight not to bask
In rich odors of crafts, cafes,
And ambling. Rather, nose to flask,
Trained as a chemist, as all ace
Perfumers did, long bitter years
Of science stinking in my face.

Just as music-besotted ears
Will cringe at noise, then so my nose
Turns up its nose at what's most dear
To it. Dear people? Those supposed
My friends amused my nose. There's why
I won't visit by phone. A rose
Or dirt is friend, too. I could buy
Myself, at whim, perfumes to sniff.
Yet, nose likes to be caught surprised.

Contrariness

The kind of mind
That zigzags. Blind
To tears, his worth's
Malicious mirth.
How it amuses
Him to confuse.

Trembler

The swaying room felt safe,
Swayed me asleep, too tired
To fear the ring of fire,
The fault, a seismic wave.

Reply

Bedazzling fireworks, my regrets, I fear
What charms my eyes would torment my poor ears.
In this, I'm seconded by terriers,
And any tender ears that clearly hear.

Once

There's music playing, plush and stumbling;
A shiver of taffeta, a steaming tumbler.

Andante

The sun has crashed in flames. Night air
Spits star sparks on the soot-black panes.
It's time I go and wander where
My face already floats, blood-drained.

Walk, silent feet, each step is synced
With breath, and into breath a tune
Sucks inwardly, and all is linked
To heart's unnoticed pulse and croon.

Stravinsky must have ridden trams.
Young Mozart felt the prissy trot
Of carriages. Beethoven and
Tchaikovsky, though, composed on foot.

Which sounds pedestrian to ears
Long sedentary, that have wrought
In music wheels and bumping gears
And cannot sense a beat without.

Don't small kids ever skip? They'll run,
And chase, and hop. Perhaps they might
Not know how to. Though any stone
Knows how to skip, you throw it right.

Try, catch the thread to sing along
With flitting birds and where to phrase
It. Tiny, weightless lungs gasp songs
Big breath can't grasp or legs keep pace.

Lapse

Pool of blue that shuns
To reflect grey skies,
Under unseen sun
Like a mirror lies,
Floats low overcast above its sapphire tiles.

Little swimming pool,
Warm as tears today,
Though the breeze shifts cool
And the clouds loom grey,
Even sundials wouldn't give the time of day.

Pretty pool, so clear,
Placid, chlorinated,
Never will be feared,
Coveted, nor hated,
As the grinding, briny, open sea that baits.

Overcast

Last night trailed asphalt-black velour, trembly
With stars. And now, at breakfast, shrugs chinchilla.

Smog

Observe, how freezing fog frosts trees and stems,
And thick fog swaddles shrinking snow banks, nights,
Or chill fog drips from ragged twigs, like rain,
Fresh fog off open waters, cut from sight.
Just so, from books, I savored London's fogs:
Clear-clanking, dank, mysterious, and cool.
Dense reader, literary fog was smog!
Foul, sulfur-yellow chimney smoke from coal.
Odd, chiming languages entranced my ears.
The bravest, richest one, clang Mandarin.
But China's smog, its suffocating fears,
Choked off a pleasantly unfocused yen.
Pollutants are revealed by smog's dark clouds.
Fog cloaks its own damp origins in shrouds.

Castle

Where thinner sunlight lingers on a ridge,
Green, backlit blades of grass, a building rich
With stone, the waxing moon. The lumpy fall
Of ground there makes it feel we stride more tall.
Or are we up on horseback in my dream?
How many horsemen rode with you between?
Maybe we walked. I dreamt this long ago,
How broad the ridge-top, and the slopes below.

Tremolo

I'd wish a home shaped like the O
In NO, that opens on its own
Internal emptiness, where grows,
In secret, moss on paving stones,
And close nearby hear water flow.

Let me compose there, coax the chords
To do what words do, grapple notes
Composers know as I know words.
My lungs fill deep. How music floats,
Though I'm no longer young—nor bored.

Dormant

White, wadded clouds, which spat and bided time,
Hung low. Coarse trees flung last leaves toward the curb,
Their bark as granite-grey as squirrel's soft fur,
Their twig stubs bare. A dullness darkened pines.
Lost leaves, once flame-bright, blown from ash-grey limbs,
Piled drifts, like crusts of bread or crusted blood,
Like clods of mud on lawns still emerald.
Blunt rains fell, loud as acorns. Now begins
To freeze. On fanned, fringed trees the first snow clings,
Sharp filigree exposing high-perched nests.
Bewildered saplings, awkward, also rest
The winter long. And all must trust in spring.
There, though you waver at long dormancy,
See, ever green in droopy sleep, fir trees.

Cliché

Could he be fond as lolling dogs to house me there,
Not pleased with his own kindnesses, nor needing care?
Could he beam smug at me, content as sun-warmed cats?
I won't have pets instead, won't be the lady that
Keeps zoo to liven the long vector of grey days
When outside's raining cats and dogs, as he might say.

Returned

Once more: damp haze and ruffling breeze;
Orange dirt; shrill insects buzz. Pale streets
Climb lazy hills. The heavy trees
And flowers flutter, lush with heat.

I feel brusque strength in frigid towns.
The northern crows croak rich and deep.
But here, I've run relaxed by sun,
Skin sauna-fresh. Here, breezes leap.

I taste the river from the sink.
Pine-shaded rooms smell musty-mint.
Slow summer ends. Tonight, I think
There're fireflies still, when headlights glint.

Beach

The tide went out, comes in. We stay. Most go.
The burning sands turn cool. The sun lies low.
Gulls elbow wind, shriek insults, flail the sky,
Shove air, since gravity can't be ignored.
Gull, Gull, you can't breathe water, weigh much more
Than air, and yet you paddle, dunk, and fly!
Fish, Fish, why care which way is upside down,
Since nothing weights you, pulls you to the ground?

Crush

That hesitating year, I loved
To catch his resonating wit.
I liked to hear him spoken of.
All others seemed too this or that.

Too dull, too fat, too cruel, too dumb.
I snubbed all tenors—he was bass.
He so mature; I very young,
And not his type in any case.

But he was my type: in his prime,
Articulate, well-tailored, fun,
And well aware of it. If time
Ran backwards, wish I could be brazen.

Chilled

One year, it barely snowed, though bitter chill,
And in the spring, spring peepers didn't peep
(Not that they ever 'peep', a deafening trill,
More like.) and clumps of bulbs had disappeared.
Another year, when harsh spring freeze froze ponds,
Bald eagles fled, abandoning their nests,
To fish in open waters. My Northland.
Like sled dogs, I loved cold air, always, best.
A blizzard is a jolting thrill, entices,
Buffets past. But how to break the ice?

Autumn Trees Haiku

Birds flown, trees tantrum,
Leaves stripped and fruit dropped to rot,
Stuck there in autumn.

Myopia

There's the site of my employment,
Which is what will pay my rent.
My immediate desire
Is to be fired.

Taunt

You gloating fool, thanks for the info.
Guess what? The only way I know
My reputation (which is lies!)
Is: you pretend to empathize.

Strings

Kites, tethered with string,
Felt not the same things
As wild birds who flew,
Though hovered those views.

White rat, the bright maze
Will dead end in cheese,
But bats in black night
Own free will, far flight.

Thunderstorm

Out, my lightning! Hush, my thunder! Doze!
Clocks are stopped. Tick-tock, the windowpane.
Hush, my wind, my hail, my patter toes!

Petals dot the pane, a spattered rose.
Puddles flood the road, a pelting rain.
Out, my lightning! Hush, my thunder! Doze!

Rumbling, roaring, dark the garden grows.
Flashing, thrashing, flat the garden's lain.
Hush, my wind, my hail, my patter toes!

Rain thumps on the roof. The maple blows.
Blow northeast, blow east, my weathervane.
Out, my lightning! Hush, my thunder! Doze!
Hush, my wind, my hail, my patter toes!

Stars

A stranger pushed a little cart.
The cart was heavy with his sacks.
He hauled along his heavy heart.
He slung his guitar on his back.

That man strummed chords to rest his feet.
He drummed a song on silver wires.
A song that rains, a song that sleets.
He warmed his fingers at a fire.

A woman wandered with a pack.
The wind was cold around her heart.
Once, when she stopped to rest her back
She met the man who pushed the cart.

They sat beside the fire in dust.
She warmed her feet. He plucked a song.
A song that swirls, a song that gusts.
The night was dark. The night was long.

He said, 'I give those stars to you.'
His fingers twanged a lilting march.
A march that soared, a march that flew.
Then fell a star above his cart.

Lost Words, 4 Sonnets

1.

His brows lift in fermatas at her whim.
She stubborns dumb. The last word, then, is his,
On this cold day when the wild sky's a fizz
Of budding trees that never will again.
His skeptic's glance. Not skeptic near enough,
He's guzzled lies as plainly as he'd sip
That glass that glosses his dry voice, won't strip
To nudity the perjuries and bluffs.
That she's here badly tried, misjudged, condemned,
But only hers all truths is useless said.
So why plaint loud and long and good as dead.
She holds her tongue, holds blurry gaze on him.
Apology? It's not her to atone.
And neither makes she epitaph for stone.

2.

A shaded dent where his lips tuck their ends.
So, there and there. Almost like sleeping child.
As snap snapdragons, his mouth too might smile
And bite, were fingers pressed into both dents.
Perhaps he's dug up earth to make a bed
For summer flowers since last week's paler skin.
Or, rather, tanned at sports and played to win.
Or picnicked with some woman that he'll wed.
She knows as certain, he's loved justice well,
And likes her not. Imagine that he slept
There where he sits and all the courtroom kept
In sculpted trance by inexplicable spell.
Then she could scamper off on skittering legs,
Flee all but life, to lie, and tramp, and beg.

3.

She'll know his shoulders' stance in silhouette
That dawn, when day turns night and he still sees.
And then he'd breakfast. Coffee. Black? Or tea?
His teeth gauge his lip's softness, unstained white.
Birds sing at dawn and slanderers sleep smug.
Once, all her doors could lock from inside out.
Or, when she left, no window left unshut.
She kept her timid nest so safe, so snug.
Here, wants brave wings, a window yet unbarred.
But she has none and there are none along
Long corridors where fear is sweet birdsong.
She asks persimmons for the eve before.
Dark jest, frost-ripened, a delay of months.
Fruits sweeter in the snow, as life near death.

4.

He smirks from out a door. His square hands clop
Her shoulders and her chest feels full of birds.
She dimples more than smiles and puzzles words.
A switch of judge? Just so. And then it's stopped?
Yes, full acquittal, brief as April snow.
Recanted lies, admitted facts, flushed tears,
Soon done. But did he hint just at her ear,
Persimmons he'll bring her himself? What? Oh,
Could he bring strawberries this summer? Last
Year's mealy apples? Box of candied orange?
Persimmons would be wiser. Now, a nudge,
A nod, and free to freedom, upward, fast.
To open doors for play, reopen doors,
And also windows, though that rains indoors.

False Fogs

Pale platinum, cold as mists, harsh, foggy beach
Where bare feet swish coarse sand, within the reach
Of overlapping foam. Or stiff, slow walks,
Sand thickly wedged in shoes, caked under socks.

Not snow here, blurring brick, asphalt, concrete.
Hallucinating, tingling, stumbling feet,
Deluded toes, assault here phantom dunes.
Cold platinum, cold as fogs, white as old moons.

Beggar's Song

I beg, for yet other Julys, again, again.
My onyx eyes
Would praise the blues of summer skies.
My gluttonous nose
Gulp madly roses.
To ramble, yet again, again.
I must come begging.

I beg, for yet another year, again, again.
My hungry ears
Might hear surf pouring froths like beers,
As pounding storms roar
From far offshore.
To listen there, again, again,
I come here begging.

Twirl Waltz

Wet snow accents each twig, like tree blossoms in April
When glanced at a distance.
Fluffy snowflakes like tutus swirl in a cold dance.
Count, soggy swan, count out twirls.

A Gentle Day

The sidewalk wafted rust
And kittens. Bikes mewed past.
A gentle day, now lost.

If **Susan Rebecca Wetmore** finds her own individualistic way in her poetry, then individualism is a family trait. The stubborn Wetmores of Kansas were descended from a brother of Prudence Crandall. Her Connecticut mother brought her ethical German-American heritage. Susan's family were living on Shaler lane in Cambridge, Massachusetts when she was born in 1954. They moved on to settle in Minnesota, Illinois, and Maryland.

Susan followed her mother and her mother's cousins to Mount Holyoke College where she received her B.A. as a discontented Art major in 1975. Later on, Susan immersed herself in the study of traditional oil painting at the Pennsylvania of the Fine Arts, graduating with a Certificate in 1985. She currently lives near Omaha, Nebraska.

Unsuccessful as a career woman, Susan has dabbled in interests in many arts and languages. She has written verses sporadically from the age of eight, becoming more focused on this endeavor now as she matures into her sixties. She has been shortlisted for the International Beverly Prize.

www.ingramcontent.com/pod-product-compliance
Lightning Source LLC
Chambersburg PA
CBHW031220090426
42740CB00009B/1243